Rediscovering Jonah Discussion Guide:

Jonah Bible Study
Small Group
Discussion Questions

Andrew Yoon Joo Lee

Version 1.0 – May, 2020

Copyright © 2020 by Yoon Joo Lee

Passages from the book of Jonah are from Rediscovering Jonah: The Secret of God's Mercy which were translated by the author, Timothy Keller.

Quotations are also from Rediscovering Jonah by Timothy Keller (page numbers are indicated at the end of each quotation).

All rights reserved, including the right of reproduction in whole or in part in any form.

Table of Contents

Introduction 4
How to Use This Guide 6
CHAPTER ONE - "Running From God" 8
CHAPTER TWO - "The World's Storms" 11
CHAPTER THREE "Who Is My Neighbor?" 14
CHAPTER FOUR - "Embracing The Other" 18
CHAPTER FIVE - "The Pattern of Love" 22
CHAPTER SIX - "Running From Grace" 25
CHAPTER SEVEN "Doing Justice, Preaching Wrath" 28
CHAPTER EIGHT - "Heart Storms" 31
CHAPTER NINE "The Character of Compassion" 35
CHAPTER TEN "Our Relationship to God's Word" 39
CHAPTER ELEVEN "Our Relationship to God's World" (Part 1) 43
CHAPTER ELEVEN "Our Relationship to God's World" (Part 2) 47
CHAPTER TWELVE "Our Relationship to God's Grace" 50
About the Author 54

Introduction

When was your last time being in a small group Bible study and thinking you were deeply enjoying the time together with others and feeling like you were actually growing as a Christian?

If you are like me (and if you have an experience of being in a small group Bible study), you probably had a variety of kinds of small group Bible study experiences. Some are absolutely engaging; discussions are deep, honest, and vulnerable, and you feel that God is alive and active among the group. Others are not so great; conversations, if existent, are mostly about facts, and often one person dominates the discussion and turns it into a sermon or devotion.

What do you think makes a great small group Bible study? What enables people of God to go deeper into the journey of discipleship that bears tangible fruit in life rather than simply gain more Bible knowledge without any change in life? There might be many different answers. I believe it starts with the leader. When the leader of the group *first* engages in her of his journey of faith genuinely and then honestly shares it with others, others are encouraged to do the same. Actually, to be more accurate, it is not that the leader must share first every single time the group meets; rather, whoever shares first happens to lead the group spiritually in that moment.

A great small group Bible study is not just about the transmission of knowledge but also about the transformation of souls; and it needs to start with an actual person in the particularities of her or his life. And when such particular story is shared with others, suddenly God becomes real.

God is always on the move; in the world, in the church, in the society, in the workplace and school, in the neighborhood, in our families, in my heart. What is He doing right now? What is God doing in His grand salvation story of humanity? And locating my story to that Big Story, what is God doing in me? Around me? Through me? Answering these questions, I believe, is one of the main purposes of small group Bible studies.

We discover what God is about through His Word. And as we dwell in His Word and consider our lives, trying to locate our stories in His Story, we discover what He is doing in our lives, and in my heart. And as we share that with others in fierce honesty as much as possible, grounded in the security of God's never-ending love and mercy, we are encouraged to obey God's will and bear fruit.

Rediscovering Jonah Discussion Guide was written with that aim in my mind. I use this for my small group Bible studies at my church, and I have been blessed with real change and growth in my walk with God myself as well as by seeing change in the lives of my brothers and sisters in Jesus. Such fruit is possible only through Jesus apart from whom we can do nothing. So, rather than trying to make growth happen on our own, we need to find God's real work in ourselves and join Him in that. This guide will help you and your group do just that.

Also, continuing to answer the question above, what else makes a great small group discussion? Good questions do. I would argue that even more important than the right answers are good questions. Moreover, God delights and uses our questions; not just those intellectual questions but also those that are visceral, those that matter to you deeply and personally. I hope and pray that you will find the questions in this guide to be an invitation to God's real work in you soaking you with His unfathomable mercy shown through the book of Jonah; that you would be able to say 'yes' to the invitation and follow and obey Him as you're upheld by others through sharing the real journey with God together.

How to Use This Guide

This guide book is for small group discussions on *Rediscovering Jonah: The Secret of God's Mercy* by Timothy Keller. You can also use it for a personal study though it may not be ideal. If you choose to do that, I recommend you keep a journal while studying on your own and also share your reflections and your spiritual journey through it with others. There is something really powerful about sharing our authentic journey in Jesus with other human beings.

The chapters in this guide are directly from the book, Rediscovering Jonah, with the same chapter numbers and titles. The participants are to be expected to have read the corresponding chapter before joining the small group discussions. If thirteen sessions (Chapter 11 is divided into two sessions in this guide) feel too long, you can divide them into two series.

The recommended duration of each small group discussion is one hour and a half, but it can be shorter or longer depending on the size of your group and the dynamic of the discussion. I suggest that instead of going through every single question one by one you lump two or three questions together and ask if people want to discuss any of them. Think ahead of time how to group questions considering the flow of the discussion. Separate the application questions since they intentionally get more personal, and give enough time for people to think and share.

One amazing way to boost engagement is for every member (or some members) to take turns in facilitating the discussions each week. On the first week, the leader can model facilitation and ask everyone else to sign up for facilitation for the remaining sessions. Whoever is scheduled to lead the next week will get to engage more deeply with the book and her or his reflection. Also, different facilitation styles tend to bring out different parts of the members, resulting in a richer and more diverse experience.

Make sure to leave some time at the end to spend time together in prayer.

It is also a good idea to have a potluck gathering in the beginning or after all the sessions are finished or between the two series.

These are my suggestions, but I am sure that there are also million other ways the small group Bible study can thrive. So, pray and ask the Holy Spirit and follow His guidance!

May God work mightily and wondrously among your small group!

Chapter One - "Running From God"

Jonah 1:1-3a

"Now the Word of the LORD came to Jonah the son of Amittai, saying, "Arise, go to Nineveh, that great city, and proclaim against her, for their evil has come up before my face." But Jonah arose to flee to Tarshish from the face of the LORD."

The Unlikely Emissary

1. How was God's word that came to Jonah unusual and stunning? Talk about three aspects: 1) Hebrew prophets, 2) the city of Nineveh, 3) Jonah the prophet.

2. Do you agree that it was unusual and stunning? Can you think of contemporary examples of similar incidents in our world and societies or in your life?

Refusing God

3. Why did Jonah refuse God's call to go to Nineveh and preach? (practical & theological)

4. Have you ever felt that God was calling you to do something that doesn't make sense? How did you respond? Have you ever refused God's call?

Mistrusting God

5. What was Jonah's real problem? What was his conclusion? After answering, read from the last paragraph of p.15 to the second paragraph of p.16.

6. Have you ever had difficulty trusting God in your life? What happened? What impact did it have on your life after that?

Two Ways of Running from God

7. What are the two different strategies for escaping from God?

"The way to avoid Jesus was to avoid sin." - Flannery O'Connor

8. Which strategy describes you more than the other? Why?

9. Though we tend to lean on one strategy over the other, we all use both strategies. What are some ways you have tried to escape from God using each strategy in your life?

10. What is the assumption that lies underneath both of these strategies of escaping God?

11. How does Jonah run from God? How does the mystery of God's mercy become the problem facing Jonah?

Applying to Our Lives Now

12. Are you running from God in any small or big way from God in your life now? How?

13. How can we become better at examining our hearts and noticing different ways we run from God?

14. What about your work/school life? Are there any ways by which you run from God in your workplace or school?

15. How can we support you in your journey of drawing closer to God every day instead of running from Him?

CHAPTER TWO - "The World's Storms"

Jonah 1:3b-4

"He went down to Joppa and, finding a ship bound for Tarshish, he paid the fare and went down into it, to go with them to Tarshish, away from the face of the LORD. But the LORD hurled a great wind upon the sea, and there was such a mighty tempest that the ship expected to break up."

"If Jonah refuses to go into a great city, he will go into a great storm. From this we learn both dismaying and comforting news." (p.23)

Storms Attached to Sin

1. What is the dismaying news? What are some examples of it mentioned in this chapter?

2. Does that mean every difficulty is the result of sin? If not, what does the Bible teach about the relationship between difficulty and sin?

3. How were the results of Jonah's disobedience different from the norm? How does sin usually operate in bringing about its consequence?

"Sin always hardens the conscience, locks you in the prison of your own defensiveness and rationalizations, and eats you up slowly from the inside." (p.26)

4. Share some of your own experiences of sin that has resulted in storms in your life. How did your (or others') sin operate in causing different storms?

Storms Attached to Sinners

5. Read this quote, "Most often the storms of life come upon us not as the consequence of a particular sin but as the unavoidable consequence of living in a fallen, troubled world" (p.27). Do you agree? What do you feel about this quote?

6. Despite the dismaying news, what is the comforting news? What are some examples in the Bible?

"And we know that in all things God works for the good of those who love him, who have been called according to his purpose." (Romans 8:28, NIV)

"The Bible does not say that every difficulty is the result of our sin—but it does teach that, for Christians, every difficulty can help reduce the power of sin over our hearts." (p.28)

7. What were some of your experiences of difficulty in your life helping reduce the power of sin over your heart?

8. Then, is difficulty or suffering inherently (essentially, fundamentally) good? Why does Keller say it is not?

How God Works Through Storms

9. What do we know now that Jonah didn't know back then?

Applying to Our Lives Now

10. In Jesus, there's mercy deep inside our storms. What are some of the storms in your life right now? What might be some signs of God's mercy inside your storm? What power of sin do you think God might be working to reduce over your heart through the storm?

11. How about at your work or school? Does your storm include them? What would it look like to embrace God's mercy in storms in your work/school? Or, how can you walk alongside your coworker/fellow students in their storms of life?

12. How can we support you in your journey through storms of life?

REDISCOVERING JONAH DISCUSSION GUIDE

Chapter Three
"Who Is My Neighbor?"

Jonah 1:5-6

"Then the mariners were terrified, and each cried out to his gods. Then they hurled the equipment in the ship into the sea to lighten it. But Jonah went down into the hold of the ship, lay down, and fell into a deep sleep. Then the captain of the mariners came to him and said, "How can you be sleeping? Arise, call out to your god! Perhaps the god will favor us, that we may not perish.""

"God cares how we believers relate to and treat people who are deeply different from us ... God wants us to treat people of different races and faiths in a way that is respectful, loving, generous, and just." (p. 32)

Jonah and the Sailors

1. How did the sailors react to the storm in contrast to the way Jonah reacted? How do they outshine Jonah? (hint: reality, concern, prayer, spiritual awareness, openness)

2. How were the sailors respectful to Jonah and his God when they found out that casting of lots fell on Jonah?

3. Have you ever been shown and surprised by nonbelievers' respect to you and/or your God? Can you recall a time when nonbelievers outshined you in their alertness to reality, concern for the common good, eagerness to pray, spiritual awareness, openness

to differences, or any other admirable qualities?

Seeking the Common Good

"[P]eople outside the community of faith have a right to evaluate the church on its commitment to the good of all." (p. 35)

4. How are believers and nonbelievers all "in the same boat"?

5. What are some biblical warrant for the world having the right to rebuke the church and for the fact that we should be concerned about not just our faith community but also for the whole human community?

6. How does this truth inform us in the ways we do our work in our workplaces and schools and live our lives in our neighborhoods and society? How about church ministries?

7. Think about your own life. If you were to be evaluated by a nonbeliever on your tangible commitments to the good of the world outside of your own circle, how high or low would you score? Why?

8. Can you think of one or two things you can start doing for the community outside of your familiar circle for the good of the public? (within this week, a couple of months, this year) Are there things we can do together as a group?

Recognizing Common Grace

9. What is common grace? What is special grace?

"Common grace means that nonbelievers often act more righteously than believers despite their lack of faith; whereas believers, filled with remaining sin, often act far worse than their right belief in God would lead us to expect. All this means Christians should be humble and respectful toward those who do not share their faith. They should be appreciative of the work of all people, knowing that nonbelievers have many things to teach them." (p. 41)

Who Is My Neighbor?

10. How does Jesus's famous parable of the Good Samaritan shed light on the common grace and common good?

11. How was Jonah the very opposite of the Good Samaritan? Why do you think Jonah lacked mercy in his attitude and actions toward others, especially those different from him?

12. How often do you identify with the Good Samaritan and with Jonah? Are there any people or groups of people who you believe don't deserve your attention, mercy, and love? Or even if you don't believe so, do you ever find yourself conducting your actions as if you do believe so?

13. How can we grow in our mercy and love toward others who are

different from us?

James 2:13-17 (NIV)

¹³ … judgment without mercy will be shown to anyone who has not been merciful. Mercy triumphs over judgment. ¹⁴ What good is it, my brothers and sisters, if someone claims to have faith but has no deeds? Can such faith save them? ¹⁵ Suppose a brother or a sister is without clothes and daily food. ¹⁶ If one of you says to them, "Go in peace; keep warm and well fed," but does nothing about their physical needs, what good is it? ¹⁷ In the same way, faith by itself, if it is not accompanied by action, is dead.

Chapter Four - "Embracing The Other"

Jonah 1:7-10

7 And they said to one another, "Come, let us cast lots, that we may know who is responsible for this calamity that has come upon us." So they cast lots, and the lot fell on Jonah. 8 Then they said to him, "Speak to us, you who are responsible for this evil which is come upon us. What is your mission and from where do you come? What is your country and of which people do you belong?" 9 And he said to them, "I am a Hebrew, and the LORD, the God of heaven, who made the sea and the dry land—he is the one I fear." 10 Then the men were seized by a great fear and—after he admitted that he was fleeing from the face of the Lord—they said to him: "How could you have done this!"

Who Are You?

1. Pair up with the person next to you and ask, "Who are you?" (Answer with as many aspects of identity as possible)

2. Think about the three identity questions: 1) "what is your mission?" (purpose), 2) "from where do you come? (place), and 3) "who are your people?" (people). What aspects of identity do they each probe?

3. Think about your answer and your partner's answer to the question, "who are you?". Did they include any of the aspects mentioned above? How did you and your partner order those different aspects? (most primary -> least)

REDISCOVERING JONAH DISCUSSION GUIDE

To ask about purpose, place, and people is an insightful way of asking, "Who are you?" (p. 46)

Whose Are You?

4. Why did the sailors ask those identity questions to Jonah? What was the most foundational layer of identity at the time?

5. What about today? What are the modern-day equivalent of Mercury (the god of commerce) and Venus (goddess of beauty)? Can you think of any other gods in our world today?

"Everyone gets an identity from something. Everyone must say to himself or herself, "I'm significant because of *This*" and "I'm acceptable because I'm welcomed by *Them*." But then whatever *This is* and whoever *They are*, these things become virtual gods to us, and the deepest truths about who we are. They become things we *must* have under any circumstances." (p. 47-48)

6. What about you? Can you think of any time when you tried to get an identify from something in this world? Are there any ways in which you're doing it now?

7. What does the Bible say about the reason why we cannot avoid worshipping something?

"[I]dentity is always rooted in the things we look toward to save us, the things to which we give ultimate allegiance. To ask, "Who are you?" is to ask, "Whose are you?" To know who you are is to know what you have given yourself to, what controls you, what you most fundamentally trust." (p. 49)

Spiritually Shallow Identity

8. What was Jonah's answer to the identity questions the sailors asked him? What does his answer tell us about Jonah's identity?

9. What are some examples of Christians today exhibiting the same attitudes with Jonah's? Why is it that professing Christians can be racists and greedy materialists, addicted to beauty and pleasure, or filled with anxiety and prone to overwork?

10. What god(s) are you more prone to seek and worship in your heart than others?

A Self-Blinding Identity

11. How is Peter similar to Jonah? What was the main cause of Peter's blindness to who he was?

12. What are the two results of an identity rooted in self rather than on Jesus?

An Excluding Identity

13. What is *othering*? When we engage in othering, why and how do we exclude others?

14. Have you engaged in othering in any way before? (Think about your family, workplace, school, neighborhood, city, the online world, and the world) Let's bring it to God in His mercy. Pray together that the power of God's grace will change our identity.

CHAPTER FIVE - "The Pattern of Love"

Jonah 1:11-17

11 Then they said to him, "What must we do to you, that the sea may become quiet for us, for the sea is more and more tempestuous?" 12 He said to them, "Lift me up and hurl me into the sea; then the sea will become quiet for you, for I declare it is on my account that this great storm has come upon you." 13 Nevertheless, the men rowed harder than ever to get back to the dry land, but they could not, for the sea grew more and more tempestuous around them. 14 Therefore they called out to the LORD, "O LORD, do not let us perish because of this man's life, and do not lay his innocent blood on us. For you, O LORD, have the power to always do what you want." 15 So they lifted up Jonah and hurled him into the sea, and at that the sea ceased from its raging. 16 Then the men were seized by a great fear of the LORD. And they offered a sacrifice to the LORD and made solemn vows. 17 And the LORD appointed a great fish to swallow up Jonah. And Jonah was in the belly of the fish three days and three nights.

"Hurl Me into the Sea"

1. Jonah changes his attitude and starts to take responsibility by saying, "Hurl me into the sea." What seems to be the cause of that?

2. Have you ever been in a situation where you're saying something similar to "You are dying for me, but I should be dying for you. I'm the one with whom God is angry. Throw me in" (p. 59)?

REDISCOVERING JONAH DISCUSSION GUIDE

The Pattern of Substitution

3. What is the truest pattern of love? What are some examples of it?

> *"True love meets the needs of the loved one no matter the cost to oneself. All life-changing love is some kind of substitutionary sacrifice. … Our loss, whether of money, time, or energy, is their gain. We decrease that they may increase. Yet in such love we are not diminished, but we become stronger, wiser, happier, and deeper." (p. 61, 62)*

4. Do you have personal experience(s) of being loved in this pattern of substitutionary sacrifice? Have you loved like that?

The Greater Than Jonah

5. How does Jonah point to Jesus? What does Jesus mean by himself being "the sign of Jonah" in Matthew 12:41?

6. How is Jesus different (and greater) than Jonah?

"The Sea Ceased from Its Raging"

7. Why does the verse of Jonah 1:15 say "raging," referring to "anger" of the storm? What do you think about God being angry?

> *"Many today find the idea of an angry God to be distasteful, even though modern people agree widely that to be passionate for justice does entail rightful anger.* To deny God's wrath upon sin not only robs us of a full view of God's holiness and justice but also can diminish our wonder, love, and praise at what it was that Jesus bore for us." (p. 65)*

8. For both Jonah's and our problem is our conviction that if we fully surrender our will to God, he will not be committed to our good and joy (p. 65). How can we know that this is a lie?

> *A God who substitutes himself for us and suffers so that we may go free is a God you can trust. Jonah mistrusted the goodness of God, but he didn't know about the cross. What is our excuse? (p. 66)*

9. Are there any areas in your life where you're struggling to trust the goodness of God right now?

-----

10. Jonah ran away from God because he did not want to go and show God's truth to wicked pagans, but that is exactly what he ends up doing (conversion of the sailors). How would you explain the irony?

11. Instead of drowning, Jonah gets saved by God through a big fish. What do you think were Jonah's thoughts and feelings when God's mysterious mercy that he finds so inexplicable and offensive turned out to be his only hope?

Chapter Six - "Running From Grace"

Jonah 1:17-2:10

17 And the LORD appointed a great fish to swallow up Jonah. And Jonah was in the belly of the fish three days and three nights. 1 Then Jonah prayed to the LORD his God from the belly of the fish, 2 saying, "I call out to the LORD, out of my distress, and he answers me; Out of the belly of Sheol I cry, and you hear my voice. 3 For you cast me into the deep, into the heart of the seas, and the flood surrounds me; All your waves and your billows pass over me. 4 Then I said, 'I am driven away from your sight; Nevertheless, I continue to gaze toward your holy temple.' 5 The waters close in over me to take my life; the abyss surrounds me; weeds are wrapped about my head. 6 To the roots of the mountains I sink. The netherworld, its bars are closed upon me forever. And yet you lift me up from the pit alive, O LORD my God. 7 Even when my life ebbs away, I remember the LORD. My prayer comes to you, to the temple of your holiness. 8 Those clinging to empty idols forfeit the grace that is theirs. 9 But I, with the voice of thanksgiving will sacrifice to you. What I have vowed I will fulfill. Salvation comes only from the LORD!" 10 And the LORD spoke to the fish, and it vomited Jonah out upon the dry land.

Where Do We Find God's Grace?

1. Where do we often find God's grace? And why?

2. Can you share your experience of finding God's grace in your life?

3. Other than simply *being* at the bottom, what else did Jonah do to begin his change?

What is God's Grace?

4. There are three spiritual truths that the doctrine of grace presupposes. What is the first one? (hint: J. I. Packer calls it our "moral ill-desert") What does the modern culture say about it? And which do you agree with?

5. What is the second spiritual truth? (hint: Packer calls it our "spiritual impotence") What does the modern culture say about it? And which do you agree with?

Amazing Grace

6. What is the third truth? (hint: costly, temple and sacrificial system)

7. What does the costly sacrifice of the Old Testament sacrificial system point to?

> *"God's grace becomes wondrous, endlessly consoling, beautiful, and humbling only when we fully believe, grasp, and remind ourselves of all three of these background truths—that we deserve nothing but condemnation, that we are utterly incapable of saving ourselves, and that God has saved us, despite our sin, at infinite cost to himself." (p. 78)*

The Shout of Grace

8. Now, why do you think we find grace not at the high points of our lives but in the valleys and depths, at the bottom?

9. For Jonah, which is the real deliverance - realization of his sin and God's grace or release from the fish? How about in our lives? Do you have an experience where God granted you a changed heart and not a changed circumstance?

10. Jonah shouts in a climactic statement, "Salvation comes only from the LORD!" (2:9). Likewise, Keller says, "Salvation belongs to God alone, to no one else. If someone is saved, it is wholly God's doing. It is not a matter of God saving you partly and you saving yourself partly. No. God saves us. We do not and cannot save ourselves" (p. 79). Do you agree? Do you ever live your life as if you do not agree? How might you live your life as if you believe that you save yourself partly as well as God does?

The Process of Grace

11. Even though Jonah goes through this amazing realization of God's grace and repentance, why is it that he explodes in anger toward God (chapter 4)?

12. In what ways do you consider your repentance to be partial and the transformation of your heart still in process? What do you think is God's current lesson for you in sanctifying you?

Chapter Seven
"Doing Justice, Preaching Wrath"

Jonah 3:1-10

1 Then the word of the LORD came to Jonah the second time, saying, 2 "Arise, go to Nineveh, that great city, and proclaim to her the message that I tell you." 3 So Jonah arose and set out for Nineveh, according to the word of the LORD. Now Nineveh was an exceedingly large city—three days' journey in breadth. 4 Jonah went a day's journey into the city and then called out, "In forty days, Nineveh shall be overthrown!" 5 And the people of Nineveh believed God. They called for a fast and put on sackcloth, from the greatest of them to the least. 6 The word reached the king of Nineveh, and he arose from his throne, stripped off his robe, covered himself with sackcloth, and sat in ashes. 7 And he cried out and issued a decree in Nineveh, on the authority of the king and nobles, saying, "By the decree of the king and his nobles: Let no man or beast, no herd or flock, taste anything. Let them not graze or drink water, 8 but let man and beast be covered with sackcloth, and let them call out with fervor to God. Let every person forsake his evil way and the violence that he plans toward others. 9 Who knows? God may relent and turn from his fierce anger, so that we may not perish." 10 When God examined their deeds, how they forsook their evil way, he renounced the disaster he had said he would do to them, and he did not carry it out.

Why Do People Repent?

1. Why do people repent? What is the example mentioned in this chapter by Keller? Can you think of more examples?

Preaching Justice

2. What was the focus of Jonah's message to Nineveh? How did Nineveh respond? How did God respond?

Preaching God's Wrath

3. Which do you think is more important - providing social services or doing evangelism? How are they connected?

4. How did the social reform of Nineveh come about? Was it through quietly doing social work, or through preaching the threat of divine judgment loudly in God's name?

> *"It is hard for us to even imagine today the ministry that happened in Nineveh. Usually those who are most concerned about working for social justice do not also stand up and speak clearly about the God of the Bible's judgment on those who do not do his will. On the other hand, those who publicly preach repentance most forcefully are not usually known for demanding justice for the oppressed. Nevertheless, this text encourages us to do both" (pp. 91-92).*

5. Which of the two aspects of the gospel message, social justice and evangelism, do you tend to emphasize more? How can we grow into being more balanced (emphasizing both)?

6. What does God's wrath look like in a society? How can we know if something happening in a society is an outworking of God's wrath or not?

> "[I]n a world created by a good God, evil and injustice are "inherently self-destructive." The resulting social disintegration "expresses [God's] wrath. He presides over the cause and effect processes he has built into creation so they are expressions of his holy rule of the world."13 That is, God has created the world so that cruelty, greed, and exploitation have natural, disintegrative consequences that are a manifestation of his anger toward evil" (p. 94).

7. Can you think of any examples in the world of yesterday and today of such outworking of God's wrath? How about in your own life? (family, school, work, neighborhood, etc.)

8. According to this biblical text, what brings about justice in society? Is it appealing to modern, secular individualism, saying, "All should be free to define their own meaning in life and moral truth"? Or is it rather calling the society to "Let [God's] justice roll down like waters, and righteousness like a mighty stream" (Amos 5:24)?

The Mystery of Mercy

9. What was Jonah's attitude when he preached God's wrath? What was Jonah's response when God responded with mercy toward the Ninevites?

10. Do you ever find yourself in similar situations as Jonah's? Have you ever "preached God's wrath" with a wrong attitude only to see that mercy was extended to those you preached against?

Chapter Eight - "Heart Storms"

Jonah 4:1-4

1 But what God did was so terrible to Jonah, that he burned with anger. 2 And he prayed to the LORD and said, "O LORD, is this not what I spoke of when I was still in my homeland? That is why I fled with haste to Tarshish; for I knew that you are a gracious and compassionate God, very patient, and abounding in steadfast love, and who also renounces plans for bringing disaster. 3 Therefore now, O LORD, please take my life from me, for to me death is better than life." 4 And the LORD said, "Is it good for you to burn with such anger?"

1. Before reading this chapter, did you know that the book of Jonah had this final and startling chapter? Did you know that the story goes on after Jonah went and preached successfully to Nineveh?

The Incredible Collapse of Jonah

2. Jonah's preaching brought about one of the most positive results in Nineveh. Then why would he melt down in furious rage?

The Theological Problem

3. What was Jonah's theological problem?

"In Jonah's mind, then, the issue is a theological one. There seems to be a contradiction between the justice of God and the love of God. "He knew that

> God loved Israel and extended his mercy to his chosen people; he felt, in the very marrow of his bones, that this special love of God . . . should not be extended to gentiles, above all to evil gentiles such as the inhabitants of Nineveh" (p. 101).

4. Do you have your own Nineveh to whom you believe God's special love should not be extended to? Who are they? And why?

The Heart Issue

5. Have you ever said in your heart, "Without that - I have no desire to go on," and/or "I won't serve you, God, if you don't give me _____?" What was it for Jonah?

> "When Jonah says, in effect, 'Without that—I have no desire to go on,'" he means he has lost something that had replaced God as the main joy, reason, and love of his life. He had a relationship with God, but there was something else he valued more. His explosive anger shows that he is willing to discard his relationship with God if he does not get this thing. When you say, 'I won't serve you, God, if you don't give me X,' then X is your true bottom line, your highest love, your real god, the thing you most trust and rest in. Here is Jonah saying to God, who should be the only real source of his meaning in life, 'I have no source of meaning!'" (pp. 101-102).

6. What should Jonah have done after Nineveh repented?

> When Christian believers care more for their own interests and security than for the good and salvation of other races and ethnicities, they are sinning like Jonah. If they value the economic and military flourishing of their country over

> *the good of the human race and the furtherance of God's work in the world, they are sinning like Jonah. Their identity is more rooted in their race and nationality than in being saved sinners and children of God. Jonah's rightful love for his country and people had become inordinate, too great, rivaling God."* (p. 104).

Misusing the Bible

7. How did Jonah use the Bible to justify his inordinate indignation, anger, and bitterness?

8. How can a devout Christian possibly use the Bible selectively to justify oneself? What does the Bible say about that?

9. How should we read the Bible? What is the central message of the Bible in this regard?

> *For what [the Bible] teaches us about ourselves is all to the effect that we are not righteous, that we have no means of justifying ourselves, that we have . . . no right to condemn others and be in the right against them, and that . . . only a gracious act of God . . . can save us. That is what Scripture teaches us, and if we stick to this, reading the Bible is useful and healthy and brings forth fruit in us"* (p. 106).

The Problem of Self-righteousness

10. Why was Jonah still susceptible to the spiritual crash even after his repentance in the belly of the great fish? What does Jonah's prayer in the fish reveal about the nature of his repentance at the

time (Jonah 2:8-9)?

11. How do we come to the place of true repentance, unlike Jonah's, so that we stop saying, "I'll obey you, Lord, *if* you give me that," but only God becomes our nonnegotiable?

12. Do you recognize the ways that you make good things into idols and ways of saving yourself? What is your one nonnegotiable you tend to hold onto even at the cost of God Himself? Let us pray God will help us bring it to the foot of the cross, crucify it, and be united with our Lord, Jesus.

Chapter Nine
"The Character of Compassion"

Jonah 4:4-11

4 And the LORD said, "Is it good for you to burn with such anger?" 5 Jonah then left the city and sat down just east of it and made a shelter for himself there. He sat under it in the shade, waiting to see what would happen to the city. 6 To deliver him from his dejection, the LORD God appointed a plant that grew rapidly up over Jonah, to be a shade over his head. And Jonah was delighted and glad for the plant. 7 But at the break of dawn the next day, God appointed a worm that attacked the plant, so that it withered. 8 And when the sun rose higher, God appointed a cutting east wind, and the sun beat down on the head of Jonah so that he was faint and weak. And he longed to die, thinking, "It is better for me to die than to live." 9 But God said to Jonah, "Is it good for you to be so angry and dejected over the plant?" And he said, "Yes, it is. I am angry and dejected enough to die." 10 And the LORD said, "You had compassion for the plant, which you did not plant, you did not make grow, and which came into being and perished in one night. 11 And should I not have compassion for Nineveh, that great city, in which there are more than 120,000 persons who do not know their right hand from their left, and so much livestock?"

The God Who Is Patient

1. We see that Jonah's conversion experience in the fish was not the end of his transformation but only the beginning. Though he received mercy from God himself, he wasn't merciful toward the Ninevites. Yet, God gently asks Jonah, "Is it good for you to burn with such anger?" What do you feel when you hear this question?

The God Who Weeps

2. What does the word "compassion" in verse 10 and 11 mean in the original language? What does that tell us about who God is?

The God Who is Generous

3. God speaks of the violent, sinful pagans of Nineveh as people "who do not know their right hand from their left" (Jonah 4:11). What is your response to this description?

4. Think about your own Nineveh, whoever in your mind that does not deserve God's mercy but only justice. How do you usually describe them?

"God looks down at people in that kind of spiritual fog, that spiritual stupidity, and he doesn't say, 'You idiots.' When we look at people who have brought trouble into their lives by their own foolishness, we say things like "Serves them right" or we mock them on social media: 'What kind of imbecile says something like this?' When we see people of the other political party defeated, we just gloat. This is all a way of detaching ourselves from them. We distance ourselves from them partly out of pride and partly because we don't want their unhappiness to be ours. God doesn't do that. Real compassion, the voluntary attachment of our heart to others, means the sadness of their condition makes us sad; it affects us. That is deeply uncomfortable, but it is the character of compassion" (p. 121).

"They Don't Know What They Are Doing"

5. While God weeps and grieves over the city of Nineveh, Jonah does not. How is Jesus the prophet Jonah should have been?

> "Here God says he is grieving over Nineveh, which means he is letting the evil of the city weigh on him. In some mysterious sense, he is suffering because of its sin. When God came into the world in Jesus Christ and went to the cross, however, he didn't experience only emotional pain but every kind of pain in unimaginable dimensions. The agonizing physical pain of the crucifixion included torture, slow suffocation, and excruciating death. Even beyond that, when Jesus hung on the cross, he underwent the infinite and most unfathomable pain of all—separation from God and all love, eternal alienation, the wages of sin. He did it all for us, out of his unimaginable compassion" (pp. 124-125).

"God Is a Complex Character"

6. Read Exodus 34:6-7. How can God be *both* compassionate *and* committed to punishing evil?

> "Why is it that God must punish sin? It's because he would not be perfectly good if he overlooked evil. But then why does God not want people to be lost? Because he's too good, in the sense of being loving. He would not be perfectly good if he just let everyone perish. So his righteousness and his love, far from being at loggerheads, are both simply functions of his goodness. He could not be infinitely and perfectly good unless he was endlessly loving and perfectly just" (p. 128).

7. We as human beings have a tendency to emphasize one aspect of God's goodness while ignoring the other. Between justice and

mercy, which do you tend to emphasize more and which do you tend to forget more?

8. How is it that we can see all the goodness of God most vividly through Jesus Christ?

The Goodness and Severity of God

9. God is too loving to destroy Jonah, and yet He is also too holy to allow Jonah to remain as he is. Do you like the idea of God who is too loving to destroy you yet too holy to allow you to remain as you are?

To be confused or angry at God is quite natural. But if we remain in that condition, as Jonah did, it will be because we do not embrace the gospel of salvation through faith in Christ alone, the gospel of which Jonah himself was a sign" (p. 133).

The Cliff-hanger

10. The book of Jonah ends with a cliff-hanger question. "For you are Jonah; I am Jonah." It is as if God shoots this arrow of a question at Jonah, but Jonah disappears, and we realize that the arrow is aimed at us. How will you answer?" (p.134)

Chapter Ten
"Our Relationship to God's Word"

Running from God (Jonah 1:1-3)

1. Keller says that all sin against God is grounded in our distrust toward God. Do you agree? Why or why not?

2. What are some reasons why we end up distrusting God?

3. Can you think of a person in the Bible who trusted God, unlike Jonah? How did that person show trust in God?

4. Share your experience of distrusting and/or trusting God in your life. What happened? And what did you do?

5. What spiritual resource do we have that can help us trust God? How can we trust God even when things are confusing and difficult?

The World's Storms (Jonah 1:3-4)

6. What are some reasons you can think of for God to allow storms in our lives? What are the two reasons Keller mentions?

7. How do you remain calm in storms in your life? What is the biggest comfort we have in all our storms?

> "There's love at the heart of our storms. If you turn to God through faith in Christ, he won't let you sink. Why not? Because the only storm that can really destroy—the storm of divine justice and judgment on sin and evil—will never come upon you. Jesus bowed his head into that ultimate storm, willingly, for you. He died, receiving the punishment for sin we deserve, so we can be pardoned when we trust in him. When you see him doing that for you, it certainly does not answer all the questions you have about your suffering. But it proves that, despite it all, he still loves you. Because he was thrown into that storm for you, you can be sure that there's love at the heart of this storm for you" (pp. 145-146).

The Pattern of Love (Jonah 1:11-17)

8. How is Jonah's story a sign of Jesus's story? What do those stories speak about the central theme of the Bible?

9. "Just as the essence of hate is murder . . . so the essence of love is self-sacrifice. . . . Murder is taking another person's life; self-sacrifice is laying down one's own" (p. 149). What do you think about this quote?

10. Why do many people complain about this definition of love in Question 9? Why is the complaint in error?

"The complaint is that it leads some to stay in abusive or exploitative relationships. However, that is to forget the whole definition. Self-sacrifice is always, as Stott says, "in the service of others." Allowing someone to exploit you or sin against you is not loving them at all. It only confirms them in their wrongful behavior and could lead to the ruin of you both. Some people do indeed allow themselves to be browbeaten and used, for many psychologically toxic reasons, all under the guise of being "self-giving." In reality it is selfish, a way to feel superior or needed. To say that self-giving love must lead to abuse and oppression is to misunderstand it entirely" (pp. 149-150).

11. How does modern, Western culture define love differently? What are some of its consequences or damage?

12. Are there any areas of your life where you're experiencing the consequences of applying the culture's definition of love instead of God's? How can you restore that relationship by starting to love as God does?

"[A]ll life-changing love is substitutionary sacrifice. We know that anybody who has ever done anything that really made a difference in our lives made a sacrifice, stepped in and gave something or paid something or bore something so we would not have to" (p. 154).

The Substitutionary Atonement of God

"The biblical gospel of atonement is of God satisfying himself by substituting himself for us. The concept of substitution may be said, then, to lie at the heart of both sin and salvation. For the essence of sin is man substituting himself for God, while the essence of salvation is God substituting himself for man. Man asserts himself against God and puts himself where only God deserves to be; God sacrifices himself for man and puts himself where only man deserves to be. Man claims prerogatives which belong to God alone; God accepts penalties which belong to man alone." - John Stott (p. 155-156)

CHAPTER ELEVEN
"Our Relationship to God's World" (Part 1)

Jonah 1:5–6

[5] Then the mariners were afraid, and each cried out to his god. And they hurled the cargo that was in the ship into the sea to lighten it for them. But Jonah had gone down into the inner part of the ship and had lain down and was fast asleep. [6] So the captain came and said to him, "What do you mean, you sleeper? Arise, call out to your god! Perhaps the god will give a thought to us, that we may not perish."

Who Is My Neighbor? (Jonah 1:5-6)

1. "One of the main concerns of the book of Jonah is that believers should respect and love their neighbors, including those of a different race and religion" (p. 157). How do Jonah contrast with the Good Samaritan (Luke 10:25-37) in this regard?

Read the parable of the Good Samaritan (Luke 10:25-37 (ESV)):

> And behold, a lawyer stood up to put him to the test, saying, "Teacher, what shall I do to inherit eternal life?" [26] He said to him, "What is written in the Law? How do you read it?" [27] And he answered, "You shall love the Lord your God with all your heart and with all your soul and with all your strength and with all your mind, and your neighbor as yourself." [28] And he said to him, "You have

answered correctly; do this, and you will live."

²⁹ But he, desiring to justify himself, said to Jesus, "And who is my neighbor?" ³⁰ Jesus replied, "A man was going down from Jerusalem to Jericho, and he fell among robbers, who stripped him and beat him and departed, leaving him half dead. ³¹ Now by chance a priest was going down that road, and when he saw him he passed by on the other side. ³² So likewise a Levite, when he came to the place and saw him, passed by on the other side. ³³ But a Samaritan, as he journeyed, came to where he was, and when he saw him, he had compassion. ³⁴ He went to him and bound up his wounds, pouring on oil and wine. Then he set him on his own animal and brought him to an inn and took care of him. ³⁵ And the next day he took out two denarii and gave them to the innkeeper, saying, 'Take care of him, and whatever more you spend, I will repay you when I come back.' ³⁶ Which of these three, do you think, proved to be a neighbor to the man who fell among the robbers?" ³⁷ He said, "The one who showed him mercy." And Jesus said to him, "You go, and do likewise."

2. Considering the parable of the Good Samaritan, how does the Bible answer the question, "Who is my neighbor?"

3. How about the question, "How should I regard my neighbor?"

4. And, "What does it mean to "love my neighbor"?"

> "He stops on the Jericho road to assist someone he does not know in spite of the self-evident peril of doing so; he gives of his own goods and money, freely, making no arrangements for reciprocation; in order to obtain care for this stranger, he enters an inn, itself a place of potential danger; and he even enters into an open-ended monetary relationship with the innkeeper, a relationship in which the chance of extortion is high" (p. 159).

5. What is the one of the bedrock truths of the Bible that is behind Jesus's parable of the Good Samaritan?

> "Each [Christian] will so consider with himself . . . a debtor to his neighbors, and that he ought in exercising kindness toward them to set no other limit than the end of his resources" (p. 161, John Calvin).

Christians and Politics

6. Do you believe Christians should be involved in politics? Why or why not?

7. Some people think Christians should transcend politics and simply preach the gospel. Why is this position impossible?

8. Some of us, Christians, identify the church itself with one set of public policies or one political party as the Christian one. Why is this harmful? (three reasons mentioned in the book)

> *"[T]houghtful Christians, all trying to obey God's call, can reasonably appear at a number of different places on the political spectrum, with loyalties to different political parties"* (p. 167).

9. How do we, as Christians, not withdraw and become apolitical nor identify with one political party compromising our Christian truths?

10. What is the only thing that can truly make us become a "good Samaritan" and be sacrificial in our love for our neighbors who we otherwise might think don't deserve love but only wrath?

Chapter Eleven
"Our Relationship to God's World" (Part 2)

Embracing the Other (Jonah 1:7-10)

1. Do you believe absolute inclusion (accept every perspective and equally affirm every kind of person) is possible? Why or why not?

2. If complete inclusion is impossible to practice, what is the new question that we need to ask?

3. How does the Christian identity enable us to embrace most fully those from whom we deeply differ?

4. Are you American, Canadian, Chinese, Korean, or whatever your nationality first and then Christian second? Or are you Christian first? Are there any other identities you put first before being Christian? Do you ever demonize people with the opposite side concerning your primary identity?

5. What is Jesus's model for loving and welcoming those who are deeply different (rather than excluding them as Other)?

"Jesus certainly had the right to exclude us, but he did not. He loved, welcomed, and reconciled us to himself—all the while not merely affirming us in some general sense but calling us to radical repentance. He neither included us as if

we had a right to be welcomed nor excluded and rejected us as our sins deserved. His voluntary sacrificial death to pay the penalty for our sins both convicts us of sin and the need to change and assures us of his love and pardon despite our flaws, at once" (p. 182).

Doing Justice, Preaching Wrath (Jonah 3:1–10): Three Lessons (on mission, cities, justice)

6. What is mission? Who is mission for?

7. What was God's logic in his argument as to why he should be deeply concerned for Nineveh? And how does that affect the way we think about cities?

8. What are two common ways Christians think about cities? What is God's approach?

"God rejects both assimilation and tribalism for his people. He forbids both blending in and withdrawal. Instead he says: This is what the Lord Almighty, the God of Israel, says to all those I carried into exile from Jerusalem to Babylon: "Build houses and settle down; plant gardens and eat what they produce. Marry and have sons and daughters; find wives for your sons and give your daughters in marriage, so that they too may have sons and daughters. Increase in number there; do not decrease. Also, seek the peace and prosperity of the city to which I have carried you into exile. Pray to the Lord for it, because if it prospers, you too will prosper" (Jeremiah 29:4–7). This must have been an enormous shock. Some of the leaders of Babylon had hands stained with the blood of the Jews' kindred. Idols and false gods filled the city. Yet God had the audacity to tell them to become deeply involved with the city, seeking its peace and prosperity, all the while not compromising on their beliefs and faithfulness

to him at all. Either withdrawal or assimilation is easier. Seeking the common good, yet without any compromise of faith and practice, is much more difficult. Yet that is God's call to his people" (pp. 191-192).

9. What does the Bible mean when it calls people to "seek justice" and "defend the oppressed" (Isaiah 1:17)?

10. How can we combine evangelism and doing justice? (explain theologically, philosophically, and practically)

11. Which of the three lessons (mission, cities, and justice) speaks the loudest to you today? And why? What do you sense God calling you to do in response to it today in your own life circumstances and contexts?

Chapter Twelve
"Our Relationship to God's Grace"

Running from Grace (Jonah 2:1-10)

1. What do you think is the main purpose of the book of Jonah? What does Keller say the main purpose is?

2. How can we stop taking sin lightly and abusing God's grace thinking "God forgives me; that's his job"?

3. What do other religions do about our burdens? What does the gospel do?

"All other religions put on people the burden of securing their own salvation, while God provides unearned salvation through his son (cf. Isaiah 46:1–4). While the gospel must lead to a changed life, it is not those changes that save you" (p. 207).

4. Why is God's grace so important?

"Whatever your problem, God solves it with his grace. God's grace abolishes guilt forever. You may be filled with regret for the past or you may be living with a sense of great failure. It doesn't matter what you have done. If you were a hundred times worse than you are, your sins would be no match for his mercy. There is a hymn that goes: "Well might the Accuser roar / Of sins that I have

> *done / I see them all and thousands more." Yet if you are in Christ, "Jehovah knoweth none."'" (p. 211).*

5. Do you know God's grace? Share your experiences of realizing and receiving God's grace in your life in a tangible way so that it deeply and fundamentally changed you.

Heart Storms (Jonah 4:1-3)

6. What does C. S. Lewis say about patriotism and antipatriotism?

7. According to Lewis, what are the two kinds of patriotism (or love of country)? How do they more or less lead to cruelty and oppression?

8. Why did Jonah's patriotism turn sour and become bigotry?

9. How can we discern whether our patriotism or passion or deep concern of anything has turned into our idols?

> *"How can we identify these "default settings" that can so distort our lives, as they did Jonah's? Look at your unanswered prayers and dreams. When God doesn't fulfill them, do you struggle with disappointment but then go on? Or do you examine yourself and learn lessons and make changes and then go on? Or do you feel that "to me death is better than life" (Jonah 4:3)? The difference can tell you if you are dealing with a normal love in your life or an idol" (p. 218).*

10. What are some of your idols in your heart today?

11. How can we be freed from our idols, self-salvations, and self-justifications which are so fragile and subject to circumstance?

"How can we be freed from our idols, self-salvations, and self-justifications, which are so fragile and subject to circumstances? Only through the grace of God, which cuts us to the quick (Acts 2:37) but lifts us higher than the heavens (Ephesians 1:3–10), grounding our happiness and identity in the unchanging love of the Father. The gospel holds out to us the prospect of a self-worth not achieved but received. While we maintain all our identifications with our race, nationality, gender, family, community, and other connections, the most fundamental thing about us is that we are sinners saved by grace. In ourselves we are lost, flawed, and undeserving, but in Christ we are completely accepted and delighted in by the one in the universe we adore the most" (p. 220).

The Character of Compassion (Jonah 4:4-11)

12. Why was God sending a deluge of disappointments to Jonah?

13. What is the mark of those who have been immersed in the grace of God?

"If your compassion is going to resemble God's, you must abandon a cozy world of self-protection. God's compassion meant he could not stay perched above the circle of the earth and simply feel bad for us. He came down, he took on a human nature, he literally stepped into our shoes and into our condition and

problems and walked with us. If you have a friend who's going through a really hard time, don't be too busy to spend time with them. Walk with them through this suffering. Of course you're going to weep. It's going to hurt! That's what God did for you" (pp. 225-226).

14. Who is one person (or a particular group of people) in your life with whom you sense God is calling you to walk in compassion even through suffering?

About the Author

Andrew Yoon Joo Lee is a missionary to international students in Greater Vancouver, British Columbia, Canada. He was born in Seoul, South Korea and moved to the United States to study abroad when he was fifteen years old. He educated at Johns Hopkins University, started his Master of Divinity at Gordon-Conwell Theological Seminary, and finished it at Regent College. He lives in Coquitlam, BC, Canada with his wife, Irene, and ministers to international students at Douglas College through International Student Ministries Canada (ISMC). He is also passionate about communal living and living missionally in the neighborhood, small group ministry and missional communities, and business as mission which all stem from *Missio Deo*, God's mission of restoring all creation into shalom.

Made in the USA
Monee, IL
05 December 2020